BAD WITH FACES

BAD WITH FACES

Sean Norton

Red Morning Press is an independent publisher of contemporary poetry. Its partners thank
Roxanne Rash and Signature Book Printing, Gaithersburg, Md.

Cover Photo: Jennifer Metsker

Library of Congress Cataloging-in-Publication Data
Library of Congress Control Number: 2005920201
Norton, Sean
Bad With Faces / By Sean Norton
p.cm
ISBN 0-9764439-0-2
I. Title

Red Morning Press
1140 Connecticut Ave., Suite 700, Washington, DC 20036
www.redmorningpress.com

Acknowledgments:

The poem "Anti-Elegy for the Self" was originally published by Poor Mojo's Almanac(k) as
"Transporter Room"

I would like to thank my poetry teachers: Robert Hill Long, Richard Tillinghast, Thylias Moss,
Alice Fulton. And a special thanks to Thomas Lynch, Anne Carson, Jason Bredle, Margaret
Lazarus Dean, Keith Taylor, Dennis Campbell and Jennifer Metsker, for their help with these
poems.

For Jennifer

CONTENTS

RESHELVING

The fact that Bialosky's *End of Desire*
        is followed on the shelf by Bidart's *Desire*

is no longer a surprise, or even quizzical.
        It is the pattern of things.

Charcoal storm clouds obscure the sun in an Indian miniature by the shelf.
        Here the enlightened ones sit patiently, between Poetry and Religion,

under the tree with the silenced name, by the milk-colored cow,
        below the split prism peacocks.

Somehow the storm cloud occupying the mortal urge
        will turn sensuously over them and disappear.

It is a shadow seen out of the corner of the eye, incidental,
        during conversation. What is left for the consort to say?

Nothing, now that the gaze has been turned inward even when looking out,
        now that the heart has been rubbed smooth as a river rock

in the underworld, now that the lotus scent is unneeded. Nothing,
        now that retraction is held out to the world of the regenerate,

who stumble on the coarse hump of nothing,
        so out of sync they may no longer falter, and falling

hear ascending notes of perfection. Skin on skin,
        The End of Desire followed again by *Desire*,

satiation followed by lack, there must be something between them,
        a confusion so small as to be superhuman.

Or is this a need like a shadow on a dark wall, a straining to be reeled in,
        a desperate desire, a vertiginous stalling before

the transformation about to happen to the unsuspecting subject?

TRANSUMPTION

> But no confusion, no disturbance rude
> Do they occasion; 'tis a pleasing chime.
> —Keats, HOW MANY BARDS

This happened when I hit the spine of Longinus' *On the Sublime* into the edge
of the metal shelf, accidentally (but there are no accidents),
where one places books to be reshelved in the section of Hindi and Sanskrit
(on the opposite shelf Bengali, Tamil, etc.) literature.

I just swung my arm forward as if to point reverently,
but as it happened absentmindedly, to what (in so many ways) I was not
able (or not yet able) to read. And the top edge
of the forest-green hardback rung into the metal,

a moderately low, sustained note. I did it again.
This time purposefully (having learned from the 'accident')
to connect these two avenues, retrace them to sound,
to one structure, architecture (one dwelling, homage, at least in theory),

to enjoy this. Thought flowed discursive and like a stream to its object,
running, like a deer past the ascetic's thatched hut. On a cover's
ink-drawn scene, where one put thumb to forefinger around one
of the infinite beads (lives, parts of lives) constituting Shiva's

necklace, the note rang out until the duration meant to create it dissolved.
A lump-in-the-throat silence: repeat twice more, flee to write down
what you can with a magnanimous sense, let the effect be weird and like frenzy.
This is the state of inspiration. Come back every day to practice,

do not let your memory confound you with forgetfulness,
prepare for numerous shipwrecks on
an eddy that assimilates a spire of both India and Longinus,
a minor abyss where the wearied gods are resting on the banks of the river undone.

WAKING UP IN THE INDIAN MINIATURE

Giant elephants ride in the night sky,
a portraiture of patience, of being
grounded in a groove that leads

to the burial ground. Against that
black velvet of night, and the purple silk
now hugging the timberline,

slow footfalls, purposeful silence, gold bells
tied with cords made from other animals.

The split of the soul that was
vapor to become flame.
The split of the mind later known to the dark.

Our minds are split
our souls are out looking:
heaven in a

fixed point, heaven-there,
heaven-grasped—loss
will drag behind you like a stone.

Little to no explanation, then lightning.

ASH TREE

Fraxinus ornus in the Greek mountains,
spooned from the bark and spread
on the belly and neck line and
fat lips of baby Zeus.

Though I never went to Athos
and did not make it to Patmos,
after I will say I drank
from the ash tree its leafy honey,

felt the honey rain on the world
from the world-ash.
I will translate some Norse mythology, not *there*,
but I suppose a here, which is as good.

Deep in the Germanic English,
as well in the Pacific Northwest,
we are said to have our appropriate worship.
It takes a long time to get to a word

like stone or tree, at least as long
as it takes to produce the actual object.
Sight fell through the tree,
that's how I knew it was the one,

the translucency. Once I found
the center, I waited breathless.
Someone tapped my shoulder
and it ended and we ate somewhere

and the world began.

DOMESTIC

I'm lifting up objects like Q-tips and toilet paper.
The Sunday news is on television, mumbling

through exigencies. The portable phone's off the stand,
battery draining.

There is a thin layer between everything.
The static of an alternate channel we're not watching.

Distant relays check normalcy, understood and taken for granted.
All the while the blood pours out of the characters of the story

and no one there would think of the little things, the Q-tips,
or triple ply, while the dead and wounded

can't marvel at the mountain's latest tantrum,
hobbling towards rebirth.

This is it, love, we've made this,
I feel the descending below us always. Some long ago,

something took us and laid us with a gentle hand
in the clay, and we feel powerless to escape.

Some long ago we were ready to kick
our way out of some long ago,

flight could have borne us home, a deluge would have been cause
for the stars, the angles of the moon, the arc of salmon,

a world ready to burn from unexpected heat. And this,
this is the cool wave that crashed over us when we turned back

to the shore and held up our hands in glee, calling out
our names to a city made of sand, where our clothes
stood, like guards at a gate, unmoved as eternity.

PAEAN TO THE NORTH AMERICAN PHOENIX

The fat-leafed jade plant shakes on the table as you draw,

pencil to sketch pad, the head of a lion
                entering a box of graham crackers. It's too dry,

the pot soil, so the plant jiggles and jostles
                as if it could hop up any minute, a neurotic,

shout it would grow no further, bite
                its thirteen green lips, and run

out of the kitchen.

I've given up on guessing where your paintings
                will lead, reconciled myself to the fact

that I can't know, I must be
                a dumb follower.

I wait, and am surprised.
                Dealing with afflatus is difficult, but who

would trade it? *All of us*, the images
                answer. And who would regain it? *All of us*.

What is the defense to a stolid background?

Tawdry backdrop of life, washed out, become
                sheen, washed over, white-washed, blue-washed, pink-

washed like faded ham hock, brown run of old meats
                and darkened egg whites on the ground gone bad.

Whoever walks there might get their legs caught
                or their thin, whimsical arms (hurrying in their detachment)

held by the bear trap that snarls,
                unconscious that it is only kept at bay by one loose nail
                            pinched into the grass.

But there, dismembered
        by a broken promise, you might see the phoenix rise
                from a box of Jell-O, young, Filipino or Chinese,

eternal, like the scribe you see now
        coming from Spain, the family line from the North.

His dark features setting to paper
        the Pacific archipelago, new President
in a foreign tongue.

The adventure of the scribe vanishes beneath
        a thick coat of white acrylic, hot dogs, Fig

Newtons are the fare across the ocean now.
        American, something from childhood onward.

Your Grandma Rose remembering the large fronds
        of dewy fern, the wooden stage of the beauty pageant.

You, remembering the long afternoon alone
        in the Jesuit chapel with dark Spanish features,

sunlight sitting in a mass just outside
        the A-framed doors, cool interior, California

like a curled lotus at the lips,
        you can't control your crying for

the childhood in California, before the wood-carved Christ.
        When will we come out to the Sierras?

In due time we'll rise above
                    the alcoholic stepfather with the pool cleaning business,

cactus needles growing out of the bark of spruce and pine.
                    The short plateau grass, narrow path out,

same breeze as the church, but here, boulders are suspect
                    in their stillness, as if suddenly

we may know in words what we've always guessed
                    was behind images, their dynamism set delicately in moss.

And because you will it,
                    a porpoise surfaces on the slate-blue water,

coursing the same way as you jog along the beach,
                    a diplomat from the polis of the sea.

The ocean's intelligence
                    looking to the land

where the species tears at itself
                    starting with the family, teeth to neck,

brutal—
                    One single person praying in motion, in league

with the sea-beast, matching speeds at a short distance.
                         God-running, showing this solitary comber
to be right in this ambition, this pursuing

that takes the mind past the pursuit.
                    Running, this is running, the creature thinks
                                        in a cartoonish bubble,

submerges into the cold nether and is gone for now.
                    The faded canvas of sand, the paper sky.

PRESENT AND ACCOUNTED FOR

The Hopi pottery piece
stolen from the site in Arizona
lies next to the arrowhead, bought
at the pawn shop, pre-Kentucky dirt still on it.
The miniature wax birthday Buddha candle,

the Polaroid of my wife reading
Auden's *City Without Walls*, New Year's Eve,
Y2K, the wound down Seth Thomas
metronome. The desire is gone
out of the event, the least nirvana.
The record is something different:

an impassible spectrum of color
applied to the senses. Are we glad
for the pause when nothing happens?
The animate members of this apartment
sit down like green leaves landing on ones
that look burned (like new delight

of expectation). The floor, the bed,
the chair, are no different than
the floor, the bed, the seat of land.
The animate members of the house stand:
the woman, the man, the cat, the oblation,
the trip to Assisi, *Exercises in Contemporary*

Grammar, Langston Hughes, *Upanishads*.
The luster is something to live with,
roiling the culture. God in her personal aspect
enjoys that the mind is formal, I think,
and that a poem in articulation has
its naturalness. With this

in mind, the shadow of a bird cut
along the back of my neck. I felt it.
Today, caught in an updraft, a leaf,
yellow as the middle way, reaches
my hand, somehow, a thing to focus on,
bring in, account for, present.

WHITE COUNTRY BLUES

A form of taxonomy:
the cursed from the cursed
into different camps.

Mojo-sapien on the left,
Homo-smokestacklightning on the right.
Now 'kick it six' and disperse

to wander this earth, there's no worse,
bouncing to the graveyard
in an old black hearse.

ANTI-ELEGY FOR THE SELF

Blank wall, forever enshrouding the further
blank walls. Precursor and plane of projection,
onto your surface the elegant fading, that felling

of feeling, that nimble nausea, mind weeding:
I drift back to the draft of other places
at the least needling it seems, a radio

or CD traces me into some other city:
San Francisco at twenty-one, peach and tan
stucco buildings, fainting by a chain-link fence;

Arizona, opening bright red eyelids to sunlight
and a giant semi hauling sheep through the desert,
gawking and stumbling towards the silver blinding mass

with nose holes, the snouts and sharp smell,
singling out a few, sticking my hand
into the cages to feel their sweaters and continue

down the dirt road from the Texaco.
Why keep these around?

FREQUENTLY ASKED QUESTIONS ABOUT STAGE LIGHTING

Am I totally lost because of the fact
that there is nothing original
in anger?

Can I slip
out of here like a dark wind
in the deepest hour: 3 am?

Do you think there is something novel
about time, that it repeats like this?
Can I speak to you at the butcher counter
in our white winter?

Have the bed bugs and mites
relaxed their grip on you,
as I did on the neighbor's roof?

Do you spend your evenings thick in the nostrils with oil?

There is hurt and not hurt,
like two frozen points on a switch,
but when do I stop moving towards the other one?

Romanov has an excellent theory about isomorphism, doesn't he?
His thoughts on luminous flux, have you read them?

Can I make it to the winter, when the
desire will even out against the white world,
and all the lupine have vanished?

I am ill at ease
by how contemporary this production is, the sashes, they appear
on the stage, an ostentation of peacocks.
Don't laugh,

that's what they are called, an ostentation, look it up.
You're hopeless, you know, don't you?

HONEYMOON AT THE SPA NEAR DEATH VALLEY

I refuse the idea that you or I will be gone.
I know I am bucking against
a vast system here, as I rest on our balcony,

against laws unfixable to notions of being
slighted. It's fair by all accounts, even
if I can't access those accounts.

I wonder if, though, this isn't about
the commentary
on the *Yoga Sutras*—

we feel scared of death because of the shame
of seeing how easy it all could've been, lighter?
It comes to us, they say, like your sister

remembers those three epidurals during childbirth,
and then the C-section. It comes to us in spades.
Insects in the mineral pools, desert bats strafing,

roadrunners hankering everywhere, tired hummingbirds
on the shaded branches. The deep summer in the deep
desert, discount prices and existential ruin. Enough.

But now I am thinking about the time I insulted my sister,
making fun of her singing at a recital, saying she was just
mouthing the words while the other girl sang out. The thought

hangs on me like the musty smell of our room, which hasn't
been fixed up since this place was Al Capone's hideout. Neither
one of us wanted to say it last night, but you can tell someone

killed a lot of people in this room, and it wasn't a comic
in from Los Angeles for a weekend. Emblematic, things
overly symbolic of the indefiniteness of new love are

infuriating. Long lawns ending in desert brush.
All the neighborhoods outside the security gates are Mad Max,
doomsday cars on blocks. Back to the astral vehicle—old time desert—

I can put some trust in the astral vehicle. *How does one let go*
of what issues forth from just being, it said in the pamphlet
from the spa treatment office here. It's always better to opt

for the smaller death of massage. I'll do well with
this little death of being married, this common prayer: If
we do go, let it not be soon. It's hard to see the horizon,

endless tracks of earth leveling dust storms made.
Subject to object, and distance, sweet distance woven in.
From now to the moon tonight, let's take it to be honey.

Honey here, honey there, honey lost in the dark.

RIVER JORDAN

You shouldn't think it's about water
when you wish to contemplate the faithful,

the deaf ones on the opposite side
keep signing there is no real water.

That's why there's the drop away of voice
and why it's troubling

when Blind Willie McTell crosses
the River Jordan on guitar alone.

We get sucker-punched each time
he doesn't sing the name but fills it

with his strings. We never learn because
there is the watery guitar that convinces us

of Jordan and the recognition
the heart feels. It must be like

the first thought after birth: this is silence,
but it contains more bliss than the world.

Elegant equations of remembrance.
It's touch-and-go the whole way across,

in fact, it's nothing but distance,
crying beyond the measured bars.

LAMENT FOR MYSELF, THE SATIRIST, THE IMITATOR

The poet reciting his poems about making,
who stopped the caterers mid-reading from making
the elaborate table at the back of the room,
because he was distracted by the making of the table
that must ultimately signal his end, his unmaking,
the end of the reading.

The tinkering, tickling drama is too much.
I am imitating his style, his drama, as I did
when I left the reading in a minor huff, at its
natural close, not noticing my own performance
until I turned off the car in front of my house.

When I was buying
gas and studying the people and their mortal habit
of being American and noisy and buying
cigarettes and driving away all in SUVs—
the name needs unpacking, un-numbing,
the vehicle within the vehicle. I didn't see how

I was still in the middle of hallucination.
His poems were a combination of hallucination
and spell casting through intensity of grief,
and repetition of grief. Then I was home and at the curb
and saw how I had borrowed that art from him—
a house within a house.

Even now I am imitating and cast myself
low for it. Unless wry humor = salvation of salvation
when equally guarded. I'm aware the core of drama,
the thing held in that makes the psyche ache,
announces its annoyance at the world troubled
by its wish to be remade.

I wish he had, upon seeing the fuss of caterers,
announced his annoyance, and then, in a guttural shouted:
"All right then, let's have it!"
That would have been uncouth, but not if he had said: "Now,
I will be uncouth, and I will shout: 'All right, let's have it!'"
Because the architecture of the space within the space,

the poet and audience within the reading
the requirement of such, would have been united, repeated.
I was home, and in my kitchen chopping up
the sheer design of my actions. I ate
celery and carrot sticks before trying to write.
I pulled out olives, cheeses, crackers, kept setting up food

on our table, until I couldn't think anymore of the
reading, consumed by food and more food,
and I shed the mockery from my intentions.
Called out, stop the Brie, stop the stone-ground crackers,
and please, please, please
stop the punch within the punch.

BEAUTY AND BLINDNESS

See Christ
walking or sitting: either going
up a small hillock or relaxing by a column.

See him
speaking, maybe because, due to movies,
especially foreign movies with voice-overs,

there is so much projection
gone into the picture.
See him

leaning somewhere, lethargic or confused.
What would it be like to be a man
who had already burned the last

stack of troubles, the whole forest
where desire lurks?

In Revelation, knowledge comes "wrapped in a cloud."
People speak of a touch, a crack
in the quotidian dirge,

but shortly after it seems
they go about as if they'd acquired
a blister from a hot pan without having noticed it.

Is this the curse, to be
at a depth catching
what you can, never remember?

I've looked into the blues, to the faithful,
but Blind Willie Johnson sings
"What is the soul of a man?" and no response

to the call, nothing from the choir. As for
blindness, the Bible is not without
examples. Two go into the ditch,

the cool mud caked on the eyes with nectared spittle.
When asked, I have to guess one might say
the worst part of being blind is reiteration.

There are moments when it is like going
over a fine food on the palette:

"It is like this, no, like this," over and over. I'd imagine
he'd say the beauty of sight would be
you are able to see through a crowd, say nothing.

SILENT POEM

Near Assisi a sign reads: "Qui morte San Francesco."

The problem with translation
is the awkwardness
of silence, what cannot be recovered.

An expression does not always press toward speech
in an ungainly way. The "silenzio" to hush
the museum crowds.

The Italians advertise Accordi e Disaccordi
(Allen's *Sweet and Lowdown*) all around Rome.

There is no wait to get into a show.

In Roma, I eat
Gelati beside a table of old nuns

in white habits. I photograph four police horses
down a dark alley and a corner

where plaster is ornamentally gummed about a fresco
of Virgin and Child. At last I feel

I have nothing to say. Actually it's been a
sneaking suspicion for a long time,

but here it is prominent.
There is nothing poor about the Capella Transitorio,

that place near Assisi, where Saint Francis died.
Its smallness alone astounds.

And there is a bit of rope.
It wants for nothing,
not even to get back to the saint.

"Nobody knows this more than me," says God.
"Assisi the unbridled," says God.

The Spanish Steps decline, full of seated tourist girls
with their purses between their feet,

whose summery pastel and earth tones
remind one quickly of the vacant house nearby,

adding Keats and Shelley to the pilgrimage
before the thunder breaks the silence over the Coliseum.

A NECTAR SCENT FROM ALL THE OBJECTS IN A ROOM

The middlebrow Classics textbook has an argument:
I feel much too dry for this assignment,
and the day I am meant to feel good,

all my teeth begin to ache and appear
to me a tiger wanting out of a cage.
The beauty coming from the Golden Age

cannot be approximated without harm.
If I go any closer
to the frieze of gods
I will be killed by the joy

turning me down. It is
mythology/cosmology/universe:
it forgets
itself, leaves you to remember.
Can we be drawn
to anything that we don't already have?

SAGE WISDOM

"It's true," you think,
"a wise person does well
in life, and a fool,
does poorly."
Then again, it's six of one,
half dozen of another
when it comes to shame.
All those things you couldn't live with
are people now,
oddly in a circle
as you asked them,
huddled clumsily.
You tell them
you want this to work, this alternative
dance class at the women's center
in Portland, Oregon,
one part Tai Chi, one part Yoga,
one part African Dance.

You want them
to be here, alert, these beginners,
but you don't feel it
or see it when you look
into their eyes.
You want them to be
the soft rising
of feathers on a heat vent,
the power of the diving halcyon,
knowing its circle of impact,
to be the fish it has
so mercifully taken.
You want that suffering
in their bellies
to come alive in Dance,
but again, they have let you down
with awkward aim

and no grace.
This pep talk goes on
for fifteen minutes,
until one of the students,
it doesn't matter which one,
wishing you weren't so uptight,
says something akin to,
one could learn a lot
from a failure.
Then, as you look
at those few faces that aren't
hung down
like the rest, you think,
"You never know
what loser is going to
come out with
sage wisdom,"
and you find you can
only step out of this circle
half-way, half begin
to live with this.

HUMILITY

Have you been to the puppet city?
The wooden slat stairs and the brown

stone stairs lead down
and around the puppet city like a lover's
arm about the waist. And above you

a castle tower looking down
on all that farm-sculptured valley. The storms
creep up, a navy blue flowering at night.

Of all the medieval wooden doors
you come upon suddenly
one is marked above the arch "humiliation."

Out come the puppets.
They hang in their appropriate places
connecting the known to the unknown.

The rain stem and roots on top of us,
the root structure to each hand and foot and neck,
taut at times, loose at others.

AWAY GAME

The worst storm of the year is nothing.

One gets beauty but not the terror you'd think

              would go along with it. "Look to the foothills

    of Mount Han," the Book of Songs keeps singing,

nature keeps at its game of pseudo-apocalypse,

        the local news still tries to tie a knot around
the vitals and keep you hooked, the harlequin

is still split and undecided and mute, the horse
            still runs in cinematic circles by the football field.
Why was there a horse by the football field?

I guess the subject of me being there as well
should be addressed.
        All I can think of when looking out across

the playing field again from high

in the bleachers, mid-afternoon, is Casey Farber,
the cheerleader I had a thing for,

        but hell, I didn't think that anything could
      explain that horse running madly in a circle
    with a huge erection. Now I would call that

"nature" or not a topic for conversation,
which are indeed the best two reasons I came up
with to say why I was there,

                had walked there, was at an away-game,
watching the fumbles and the missed kicks
                        and the awkward but eventual scoring, instead

                    of hanging out with the rest of the skaters
in my basement listening to Suicidal Tendencies.
What a curious thing to have been alone at all.

Rage on 1986, rage on pathos of adolescence,

you can't help but rule over the spiritually
                    unfulfilled. You don't have to wait

now for news until 11. Get it at 10, chomping at
                    the bit. The local circle of confusion,

if once taken for granted may become an un-maddened straight line,

a protuberance out of the day, unfolding gingerly: cascading
clops of snow, the huff from the nose, the built up
steam moving us forward.

PICNIC ON THE HIGH SEAS

Like most I wanted happiness and truth.
As happiness stretched out ahead in the waters,
dimly, almost without image,
I started wanting it more than truth,
and then when it was clearly over the horizon
I wanted it from the one or thing
right next to me in the boat.
                        It was a nice
wooden craft, sailed well, or had
so far. Had a solid belt of iron.
The water was relatively steady with
a thin plane of fog off it. Confederate
colored water. The Atlantic, without
storm. I didn't know such a small craft
could make it out this far.
                        No bellyaching,
sit down, the lunch is in the box.
No, I didn't get these shoes in New York.
The slacks? Yeah. The quiet is nice.
I put that *Spanish Lullaby* on the tape
I made for the trip. I'm not sure, 1913
I think. Do you have any soap?
                        Once,
I was in Seattle, and some monks came in
on a radio station. That was nice,
trying to listen through the static for it.
One of the monks had been a surfer
in a different incarnation. Oh, whoops,
I dropped the roast beef, who's was that?
Nikolai, it's in the box!

Mustard!

He said he remembered when he'd
rush in, but then he aged and it was
one toe and then another toe. His advice?
The other monk just said, "You've been
set up," and then asked us how
we felt about it. I suffer from noun hunger.
Yet all the parts are in
their places.

THE CLEANSE

First image: a being prefigured as an angel walks away
postfigured as a broken thing, an elaborate

puppet with its gesturing hands reaching back
trying to affix the wings. Cruelty's afoot

and it's time to let it go.

A child forcefully constructing a windmill toy—
missed opportunities.

The next image: a child sitting in front of a fire,
age 6, reinventing narrative in the shadows of flame,

could be anyone in there, could be any feeling in there.
Because of how little brain space used, and all that's

stuffed in, every time an American walks out of a building
87% of their mind is watching the thing blow up

behind them, and the possibility of them either being
the hero that rides the wave or the extra. (I got the next image

from the movies too. Antibiotics really threw
me for a loop). The other 13% is on the store, the lost thing.

By age 26, one's a child still reinventing the factual world
and is thoroughly annoyed by statistics but flagrantly in love

with theorists. It's embarrassing, don't think about it too much,
send it out the back door with some pig latin.

A relatively quiet day with a solid pain in the gut.
Let's make up for all the lost time if we can. A light fixture

in the kitchen ceiling makes me feel like an early teen,
someone yet to be scrambled. Save me from the eggs image.

The fear afoot, the shame afoot, yes, more anger,
the sarcasm afoot, miles and miles and miles.

No image, just the chasm, it's there, the lit-darkness, go, go, go.
The last image: where these worldly eyes can't see.

JENNIFER AT RETREAT

I grow to the interior and forecast a root
reaching sideways to touch a warm stone.

Before making it through the tunneling of dirt,
the chill comes down like a mouth on my mouth.

At other times a dream comes and goes without words.
A flat vision, television-like, of a vibrant auburn

hanging from the trained slenderness of young birches,
which guard the path to the horizon.

Remember who I am. I am hanging
on the edge of walking into a perfect season, horizontal,

intimating God and not having to believe in the theological sense
because I know damn well...

Even now I am not able to mention it without the feeling
of shame, the isolation of small talk, the knowing

through doors, behind walls, verticality,
things fly loose, play it loose, don't aim up, shake down, empty out.

THIRST: DESERT OR GARDEN? *(Pasadena 1880)*

The imagined world wants to be by a clear
flowing that sounds not far off.

Where the water wants to slip over
auburn ground—
what longing water has for places,

unnamed places. It'll wait somewhere,
but not for long.
Who would chance losing this?
Hazard a greater ecology than

the city with its big,
dour smile, paved? Trade of the mind
traffics but doesn't prosper, you have

nothing once the ability of this waterway
is gone. I hate to even picture it, yet I
can. A dark field below the punctuating moon.

JESS ON RETREAT

Great ideas don't come in flocks,
so the mountaintop has become essential.
Something touched is reworked internally.
No one learns from flowers unless directed.
That direction comes from within.
Great ideas may infuse rivers,
and therefore bathers may be insinuated.
Cold months seem unbearable,
and hot months, unable to withstand,
all these times are accustoming.
One little thing is to preserve order.
When there is something to do, do it,
or wish you could do more, or don't wish.
I thought it bore itself out in breathing.
Tape cassettes still hold a great deal.
Trying to slow down, waste little.
Black ink is not blood. Metaphors abound.

I'M GEORGE EASTMAN, AND I NEVER LEFT YOU

Those little people must hate it,
dressed up, in their burgundy cars
and chartreuse business suits, for Sunday worship
or leading the tour of the Eastman House.
The nefarious woman who brings the fourth grade
into the last, broad room, with shockingly white cornices
embedded in the four corners—one for each season—
says, "This is where, George Eastman, writing

'I have finished my life's work,' killed himself
by shooting himself in the head." I am with those
factory workers and washers for clothes lines,
flockers to suburbs, hinterlands. The center
didn't hold, since they buried
the flour mill wheels, dug apart some earth,
called Rochester the "Flower City" and laid down
numerous lilac bushes annually succoring
the favor of German tourists and lovers
of the snow cone and sausage. The earliest wheel

was recently found between the cragged shells
of buildings around High Falls in the High Falls district.
Again I look down on it, the hand crafted
brass and iron, the ossified wood highly functional,
more so than Xerox moving their consultants
to Connecticut or Bausch & Lomb manufacturing
the same contact lens and selling it as three different ones,
at ascending prices. People throw out sight
that would've lasted them 6 more months, each week

emptying the waste of perfected eyes into the mud.
The Genesee chaotically flows northward like the Nile,
harbors no Moses as it should, spilling its waste,
human and industrial, into Lake Ontario, suspicious
Toronto haunting the other side. I never went anywhere
from here. Though I have tried, I wake up in the violin case

in the third row of the Rochester Philharmonic
ten minutes before the performance, a beta-blocker
skipping over the dead stones of my teeth because I'm nervous.
I weep with the soloist's rendition of Paganini.
I comically portray myself as the disfigured giant,
demon-genius producing the inhumanly crafted image,
shadow man in thick topcoat and beard, long hair strung

from the backs of ravens. That odd portrait hangs in
the concert gift shop. I pretend that I am taller. Or that I
am invisible, or that everyone shuns me. I shunt through
Highland Park in the off season and mock my own face
beside the broad, chiseled nobility of Frederick Douglass,
the statue, without plaque, subject to Frisbees and pot-smoke.
Sick of seeming wicked and woebegone, I hop the wrought

iron fence of St. Mary's into the prayer garden,
St. Mary of the Highways, 390 rushing behind her, her arms
holding the child with devout precision, for this eternity.
I dream the crucified man's open limbs, something she
must have assumed. I read to her from a library book
of Pasternak's poems, telling her of his Magdalene
then how quickly this ice will melt when the humid days come,

how Africa felt the first time, why the elephant at a long look
doesn't deserve to be hunted, its limbs cocked
with its great memory, kicking up the dry, tan dirt,
charging your bullet in mid-flight, killing itself with your bullet,
before it crosses some imagined but no less real boundary.
From here back is mine, and over there, yours.
We both know death must occur and will happen here today.

I'm not sure why I've told her all this. It seems like a lie.
Over my shoulder I see the street dusted with light snow.
I feel cold and think of myself disappearing over amber trees,
into the black light behind them. Chatter of passers by
is the negativity of chemicals swishing in the trays
of glass windows lodged in the building frames,
a silver liquid that lets nothing through.

FIRENZE WRITING WORKSHOP FOR THE NEWLY DECEASED

How did Dante know
this was the threshing floor
that drove men mad?
How did he, exhausted, resting
on the church brick, decide, as he did,
to make the quotidian infernal?

Everything is made of tin here.
The Duomo is a paper house.
Another alley to the Arno, a fourth
or fifth broken payphone, the static
or worse, no tone at all.

The wire holds my head to the orange box.
It is not disrespect but frustration
that damns places, people
one half step past their limits,
without tether. It never goes unwarned:

in Roma, in the Vatican,
the conquering of death must come
with a price, a continual reminder
to be silent, to not take pictures.
I agree to both injunctions,
no idle words, no structures
to take with me when I go.

TO THE BOY AT 5 FIDDLERS LANE

Let me remind you, young friend,
about homework. Homework comes in threes:
retail marketing should be made more efficient,
the joyousness of service is often very hidden,
the eagle flies at midnight. The last,
as you've guessed, is your ticket outta here!
The two former are your return ticket
to 5 Fiddlers Lane, where all those forlorn
fiddlers flood back, with their sacks and sashes
and bloodied noses. But I'm not saying
don't fiddle, young fiddler. You must play
through the pain if you're from 5 Fiddlers Lane.
The Latham Chamber of Commerce
would like to inform you the individual
golf package can be merged with the day
at the track. The horse named Roses
once having been ridden into the sun
now bares many scars yet little effulgence.
Ready-witted boy, feel free to hate
this warning. A boy must live a long time
with just his own circumnavigating thoughts
to fashion a sophisticated passport out of them.

—for D.C.

40

COMMUTE

By Logan Square I see the "Magikist" sign
above a turned-off factory
rising out of the trunk of morning,
a large pair of metal lips
the size of a house.

       I will count the bulbs that wind
around the upper lip and part the two lips and pull
the lower down with or without power.

As the train descends into the tunnel
I will not think
about the knob that you
pull down in case of an emergency that looks like
a swollen red testicle.

I will be as far away
from thinking thinking about thinking
as I have always been

       as far away as the sign at the next stop that reads
"What-can-we-do-for-you-today?"
"What-can-we-do-for-you-
today" long past when today has disappeared from sight.

EYE AND TONGUE

You take the goat's eye and I will take
the goat's tongue, said Vassilis, as we relaxed
at an outside table in front of the Bush Café, Tirana.

This is how village Albanians insist on someone
beginning a feast. The old men
and the young men and the old women

and the young and the little waif children
and the heavyset children and the museum
of cultural artifacts and the strange promise

of the super technologically advanced manual
typewriter that panned some gold that was lost
in a ponzi scheme that led to rocks being thrown

mostly by young men and old men and boys
like myself by the end of the month of May in Tirana,
I said. The NY Times had covered it, back

when the front page was black and white.
We both had it on our refrigerators then, in '97.
Every tightly knit group needs an outside enemy to be

tightly knit, Vassilis said, becoming more familiar.
Everyone suffers within stone walls with a dictator's
name written outside them in white paint that no boy

can touch and no manual typewriter, no matter
its refinement, can type black ink to equal
or type red to edit, or type white correction

to mock its despotic scrawl. But
I was not sure if this was so, the other men
in the photograph looked just like me, and the rocks

were aimed at the elected cabinet, the enemy
squarely in range and within. O Vassilis,
I said, do you see what woe and liberation

I've seen during this meal? Yes, I do, he said,
people have an odd ability
to be captured.

IN THE BELLY OF THE WHALE

Every day Steve drives the city bus.
Morning or gloaming he drives, textbook style.
With the shower of Seattle on continuous.
At the stop light another bus

rounding the corner. Here comes the whale
out of last night's PBS documentary.
We are under the deep Sound,
so close to the mythic beast, within

our imitation whale constructed for these
Aqua-purposes. The wild is underrepresented,
so we needed to fashion this pretense
of whale and this camouflage of being.

Suddenly a man in the back seats realizes
he meant to take the 10 to work in Pioneer
Square, and not the whale to the depths (for
Science!), but it's too late, the depths make him

lose his place in the middle of reading
the book he has of the author
he is to introduce tonight at Elliott Bay,
he senses that abruptly his heart chakra

is awakening, and a large imaginary flower
is stop-action-film-ic in its public
domain. And the calmness of this
is supported by the fact that Steve is now

driving the whale, down toward the sound
of morning deep beneath the foothills
and switchbacks ascending the Olympics
and Cascades. Another whale goes by.

The ethnomusicologist turned oceanographer
reaches for her walkman that when spoken
into receives the subtle transmission
the great mammal has been trying so long

to be able to speak and therefore forget forever,
the laborious and slow-moving gravity of self.

UNDERWORLD ADVERTISEMENT: FOR JAMES WRIGHT AT 32

You will only live twenty years more
and then you will go down in the afternoon
of oblivion.

With all you know, you might
be happy there, after all,
at times

you've found happiness here
in the broad face of the moon
on a noble, invisible spine,

hiding in the fields of darkness that harmed
no one. In the underworld,
I see your hands

going into the loose clay and olive refuse
wondering who went this way
and why.

There is a solitary star, pale and descending,
the thick mist like rouge against its setting,
while you play a single plainsman pulling an arrowhead

from the tough neck of a beech tree
by a cursed river, outside Minneapolis.
But you won't be alone for long, in fact there'll be crowds

that you'll have to
balance precariously, on one flower
or corn stalk, to make disappear, and yourself with them.

It's worth the effort
to become inviolate, to watch your hands
veer into the muddy folds of landscape,

silent as twilight,
or to come back dressed
in Depression Era rags or football uniforms,

as Ohio itself,
pliant and protean, the land
that you sweep off the Midwest's

flat table
and call back again,
pacific and redeemed and unbroken.

JOURNAL ENTRY: BEAR RIVER WRITERS COLONY

The raptors on the fourth day maintain unnatural poise. Old woman prays with hands not touching maple syrup. Man says, "She's praying." There's something wooly. Changing in the dim light you are suddenly naked by the metal of the kid's camp bed. It's morning—there is heaviness and heat—and the large hand-carved boats are coming ashore behind me. I'm outside. The thick blue curtains have yellow crescent moons campers painted on them and then got high or unbelievably queasy at the thought of your sex, or their sex, or fishing worms. The boats are ashore now. The Ojibwa Indian families in one line to the dining hall. The swan outstretched the wolf teeth bared the squirrel forever planning rich winter, nailed to the rafters. The old woman is there praying, now. She's praying. Now. Their arrival is coincident with the raptors. No one notices except the high school kids from the remedial school who feverishly publish these thoughts for the last night's reading. The poet laureate of oak and ash and horse awoke one day on the other side of mourning, shocked somewhat by the truth he'd been carrying around chest-high and articulating these many years since the first short story didn't guarantee career, and the death-truth suddenly had stolen out of a cancer poem he'd published against himself. It drove off with his bride, and love moved in and when such love opened his suitcase and the poet looked beyond the gauzy and tattered divider, he took no notice of the hand mirror or the antique sneakers. He was branded with dismay to find a sash that read 'surprise,' in his handwriting, mortified when he found himself putting it on, its red cloth disappearing on his flesh. The boys on the shore play with trout. The high school kids can't even see the electric ghost he's become beneath the surface of things. He evades campfire stories. The tired bacon goes to mouth. In favor of noon garden chats. She's praying. People keep handling the reverence and the birds remarkably well, but she's still praying. When will she come outside? When will she come outside so we can eat lunch at the same time?

DAYS OF REST

Blanched walls coated by an easy
listening station,
picture windows, flat perspective
from the 8th floor, goldenrod,
flush in the median.

Hands of euchre shuffle and deal
an open field. We are all a little quiet,
we are all a little lost.

The intake nurse's hands look bruised
by the ink of her pen. The waiting window
is cloudy, an industrial mistake
until it took its own form.

Her face is as thin and pink
as a pomegranate seed, her voice
like wind over a stone. She says visiting hours

ended at 8 pm, the doctor you need
can't be in until Monday.

You are free to stay if you like.

I think it over so long
I come back to the beginning
to find a breezy piece of mindstuff
I didn't recognize.

I pace through
and through the night.
The floor moves its iron lung.
Dust bunnies gather at the static
of my hands.

THE ALLEGORY OF BAD GOVERNMENT
—On Ambrogio Lorenzetti's *Allegoria del Cattivo Governo*

I was dumbstruck
by the emptiness at my chest
which can be described as the lack of
foreshortening. I stood
at the bower and in the mud, before the descent
wondering at the truth of the situation,
what the commotion of gold and clouds
could add up to, visually.
Before the considerations of what was really
knowable I shuddered, not because I thought
the question itself was profound,
but because of the utter waste of time.
I could "see" the waster of time as
headlights shot into the air made
prominent by the gold sky fading to a
violent-blue. Not an attractive image—
headlights shot into such a night as this.
And who drove that car, and rode with him,
lasts only as concerns of the myopic.
It was the prince and the baron if you want
to know, and they never returned
that night, like Constantine or Reagan,
or the empire that plodded along.

—for J.Z.

AT A FRIEND'S CABIN AFTER THE POET'S FIRST DIVORCE

Now, I've brought up all kinds
of spices, and I can't think what
they were meant for. The faucet's rush
sounds identical to the grill cooking, the hiss

and blankness in between the hiss.
It hurts so much it could crawl into
a ball. That's what the cooking food
is saying, or what comes out in the oil.

Now, both are going, the water and pan,
and flame is contending with its enemy,
and both are hot, and the steam
rolls and hangs in the middle sky,

as I am no more than listening
to my own food chastising me
for knowing so little and consuming
so often anyway. Who says we have

to know anything to get by, I ask;
but the lack of human speech in response
is enough of an answer even for an idiot
like me. Who says fowl versus fish,

sky seasons earth?

TAPESTRY

The hand slung down water-ward over the brocade,
the hand bloated and uncommemorative. The view of the scalp,
and not the eyes which no longer functioning can't balance against
the rock of the small vessel as it sits gingerly in dock.

> All the faces from the long and weathered march
> skipped April, May, June, July and went straight
> into August.

A charcoal mist feathers in from the East.
If it is daytime, then the war being on the cannon soot has polluted the air
If it is morning, the gray mask of industry is being slowly fitted to the face
If it is dusk, the world is being sloughed off in a frustrated mass like a leaden
shroud.

> The grainy light that makes it off the bed robes under overcoats
> mingles pugnaciously in the mind with the anise
> that fills the nostrils with its wet sweetness, that reminds

few of childhood amongst the men in derbies and the women wearing kohl.
A hurricane lamp is brought from the shelter and held out into the thick.

Ladybugs take to the sky in thousands. Millipedes cover the ground,
a translucent gray-green wave like the onset of nausea.

Children carry around small pieces of slate with Xs and Ys printed on them
occasionally running into one another and creating two dimensions,
occasionally coming upon each other like chromosomes ready to submit
to the unforeseen pattern coughing in the wings.

Death, untimely death, is bound to make people nervous, nobody wants
to hear that the hero was really a bench warmer. It makes us all a little sick inside
with bad news.

It is said that sport should go well with nature, that nothing should be done
for entertainment that, say, doesn't fit with standing outdoors approaching
the distant stars. Maybe it's wrong to think of entertainment at a time like this,
but carnage has seemed to fit with the stars, the pluck of nature

even in the torn revelation of a bird, the release of this town or that town on this or
that hillside, in the silky cords of fire, in the fabric sown, albeit with a beautiful effect,
by hands that learned to mimic the weave.

THRENODY: ON A FINAL LEAVE WITH MY FATHER

Just a thin sliver of gray blue on the edge of the rock face.
He is lying on his side.
High cliffs, everything is wrinkled and tan.
No one can walk this far and not feel existentially akin to twilight.
A stubborn twilight had stayed in his system
for fifteen years, ever since his father
told him about his time in Germany
on leave in the Black Forest.
Often when he was with his father now, he imagined him
lost and gaining mystical understanding.
The hotel room was red enough with electric sign
that the twilight of insomnia made belief in simple noise heroic.
He laid on his side with the static, his father in the other bed.
Lean into the forest now coughing, he instructed himself.
Nature doesn't say the whole thing on purpose.
Phlegm in the forest, diabetes roots.
Stay until you deserve passport over the gulf
between self and sky, he'd concluded.
One day soon on the other side of this underbrush
twilight will ease out of summer,
so he can ease himself into a warm half-sleep
until sight grows subliminal then superlative.
No matter how many times there will be the darkness and the sun.

RETURN OF THE MOUNTAIN LION

I have not looked long enough
at the green pea tarnished with boiled egg slither
to see how to laugh.
Because my words failed it,
no one could say beauty.
It was a horrible law, not a law really.
I can admit that. Don't you watch the game
on the corner of 54th and T.V.? Every
Thursday there's another.
We call it pain.
Every window—that's an exaggeration—
just one, read, Leave Your Pain.
A glass door, and I opened it for others,
and read the slogan aloud, knowingly,
and pointedly, and walked through myself
but nothing changed. Converted to change,
all those dollar bills and dollar coins,
now hope in a paper cup. I walked
through myself for miles until
54th and T.V., and realized I'd gone
too far and needed to head back
the dusty road to the family
slaughterhouse.

NO TUBA

It's not as if we heard the music and recoiled.
Or that the quality of air in the summer street
wasn't enough on the way home. The whole

day the beach was swarming with magpies and
children. I don't swim much, you swim much, it

was time for Frisbee. When I spoke to the man

from the tuba ensemble he said people weren't
ashamed and there were forty or so of them.

Most don't know how to handle children on
the gray chopping lake waves, they make
them odd hovercrafts and toss them or bend

them like screaming fish, backwards, laughing in fear.
Few give trident rebuff: namely, consequence.

Better to know of it and sink down

until only the head can be above the water
and watching mark the land. That's my bag

on the beach by the guy in the Speedo and lime
green hat, and surely overcompensation is a sport,
why else would they encircle her suggesting

it's never too early to make the day die down,
a darkness around me shaped like a tuba.

YOU DON'T TAKE THE BITTER HERB FOR YOUR RHEUMATISM?

Said my grandmother from the corner of the room.
Melvin Arndt from Arndt Funeral Home
walks in and shakes out his black umbrella
with a wooden duck head handle
that appears to have pink lipstick
across the bill. And no surprise it falls
neatly into the antique, and the residual
moisture sound like the noise
from the back of Carla's throat
as she chokes on a pretzel, laughing
alone at a movie that she directs herself.
The second hand on the clock
works as a prop to hold the body up
as long as it can. It circles,
and is mistaken for a heron,
also wearing pink nail polish.
My grandmother who is not quiet
any longer, is at last memory
carrying its own luggage.
A suburban bay window looks as if
it could be eaten at once and put down whole,
a cold sandwich, a light November
afternoon rain, special effects.
The hand circles again and is mistaken for
food on a spoon, a bank clock, industrial clock,
outdoor promenade, by my grandmother.
Pink nail polish I believe
may look like candy.
She is not quiet in any way as she spirits
an imaginary friend, who is the last one alive,
the last one to make it out of her in one piece.
He dances his way to the appointed place,
Holly, NY, 1952, 1952,
waiting to be picked up by the next car
out of her mouth.

FACTORIES LEFT TO THEIR OWN DEVICES

What should we do, she said,
now that we have to be factories
of first things?

His fingers and his limbs
went numb from pressing buttons.
Then his limbs disappeared
as images dodged on the screen,
and then his eyes, and then black.

This is the same as a 500Mghz
chip can do, she thought. It is not surrender,
it is dropping away. It is a
heart attack.

And he was gone, replaced by a moving
van, items marked by room,
bubble wrap, and numbers where she
could be reached.

She can't
keep up. Finishing a conversation
is occluded by a new necessity.
That's technology.

Again, her son huffed, unable to bear
the recurrence. There's nothing left
to do. She answered her own question,
might as well just press on.

RENUNCIATION ON RETREAT

I put everything in a sack
and carry it down to the lake.
The bowl that had been used
for cereal tossed in first.
Then the copy of Gide's
The Immoralist. The purple
corduroys and the long
underwear shirt float
the most. Occasionally,
a white mouth will
lift out of the gray water
and try to bite the edge
of something. The first
writing journal sinks, no
problem. "Horticulture,"
and "The flowers of Paraguay,"
written on the back
of a bank receipt offered up,
go down. 80s punk
and 60s Free Jazz say up yours
in the modal waves. CDs
bob like rainbow
lures broken from a line.
A spoon carries the murky sky
down to the sand and pries
it in past the closed-mouthed
rocks. Knowing how to free
oneself is nothing; it's wanting
it that is hard. The gray waters keep
bubbling with the breath
of increase.

PUCKERED AND SHOOK ON LOWER HAIGHT

The room we fell into was the one
in which we slept on one mattress,
four of us. One guy wore his army boots
to bed, and for that matter, all his clothes, so he could
get up at five and walk out the door to work.

He worked as we all did at a health food store,
whose produce was often no different than the Safeway's
across the street except a dollar more a bunch or pound.
My boss's name was Edward. He was an alcoholic
but fair in that he had hired me with blue hair,

no references, a nervous stutter. He soon proved
an oaf. He would say be back in a minute
then call three hours later. A Nob Hill bar surrounded him
like a warm bath. It slurred his words. He said, "If my wife
calls, tell her I went to the bank." But it would be 8 am,

on a Sunday. When he never showed I'd get out the padlock,
chains and close up. Back at home I found
the boy who slept in his clothes reeling in a corner.
When I propped him up he said that he had eaten off
a plate on which Jim, our fried hippy friend, had cut up acid.

We stayed up most of the night, *almost* staring at each other.
He was looking blankly at the cream-colored wall.
I was looking out the window at a single streetlight.
I'd look away for fifteen minutes and then look back
and ask him a question: What is going on outside?

Then I'd look to see. At around 3 someone else
came home and looked in, asked what'd happened.
I dosed him, I said, laced his peanut butter sandwich.
For a second the dosed kid's face puckered and shook,
and he seemed to almost believe what I'd said,

and admitted later that's what caused him to lunge
and hug me. His depth perception must've been off
because he launched into me without thought of the wall,
its meticulous cream, and his head smashed into it.
I was so surprised that I almost didn't notice the blood

from my nose that covered my shirt, from where his shoulder
cut across my face as he performed his albatross flight.
Enough, the newcomer in the hall said, and went to shave
his head. Jim came in and told me to snort some Vitamin E,
or was it Daniel, another fried hippy, just in from Marin.

It wasn't Punk Daniel, the other Dan, he was always out till dawn.
Back in 1990 the Gulf War was starting up or being planned
so each morning after the guy got up to go to work,
Punk Daniel would rush in from the living room playing
"Praise God and Pass the Ammunition," making us get up

to thrash about the room. These were our calisthenics.
Later, when I moved up north, I heard from a friend
about some guy called Punk Dan because he was present
at every show. A month or two later he drowned at night
in a small Oregon lake when he fell out of a boat.

I didn't ever stop to think there may have been a service.
It seemed less absurd to think Dan was at the bottom
of a forest lake or bog, nightly becoming petrified
than to imagine a man had to strip off his boots and kilt
and slip him transmogrified into a suit, for parishioners.

For who? It was these small details that we had no idea of
in regards to each other, who we each belonged to.
One day right after I heard we were in the same town
again, I'd found him at an outdoor concert
dancing on top of a trash can. He was bone-thin and had

a permanent shake to him, but he remembered me fine
and wanted to be remembered to everyone else.
Where they were, I had no guess. That also was fine.
He wanted to talk about the day
he was followed in for morning exercises by the house cat

who promptly began spilling kittens in a wavy line on the floor.
We had done our best to guide her into the closet
and to lay her down on a T-shirt. Someone had searched
the hall, finding a few more and we put their moist bodies
with the others against her tender belly. We all got home

around the same time that night and stood before the closet
without a door, an otherwise empty space, and quietly looked
down on the image of the mother and children. She had

eaten a few of them during the day. We agreed, though,
that she was probably done and as a matter of course
decided not to prevent the others from sleeping on.

HONEYDEW

1.
We got a jump from the attendant at the front gate
and the woman I was with slept beside the sleeping dog

and the gears popped in and out.
She talked about going to the Oregon Dunes
but I said

dune buggies
seem like mall culture on speed.
We had been fated
not to make it. You'd think I would've known that.

2.
Perennial Oregon overcast.
Though she'd been here before
I asked her to not tell me
what the place was like.

The same Pacific as on earlier stops,
fogged over under such a prematurely darkened sky.
It looked like a tidal pool,
a twin to an actual tidal pool

that seeped in front of a tall rock face. The flat, gothic wall
spread along the coastline, reached up into the low fog and all.

3.
It blocked the ocean. It was like a long flung-out panel
that might've had Rogier van der Weyden's *Last Judgment
Altarpiece* on it, with its nearly caricatured aurora, except
this was more like a scene three weeks after apocalypse.

"Had enough of this?" she said, and I wasn't sure what she meant.
At first was thinking, *of Oregon*? But that sounded funny.
I just moved here a week ago to be with her. I almost answered,
but then I knew that she meant us.

4.
A kid with a honeydew melon larger than his head
sat on a craggy rock trying to manage the inside,
pale-green flesh with a plastic spoon. His feet
were immersed in the mist which now clung mostly

to the surface of the pool, and every time he missed the mark
with the melon a chunk fell at his feet through
what looked like loose cotton balls around his ankles.
"What's going on?"

he said, mistaking me for a family member. I wanted
to say, "what in hell are you supposed to be?" But instead I said
"what do you usually do?" "I play, I'm a kid," and
he scampered off somewhere into a cloud, having dropped the melon

which made a sound like something soft and full and easy.

BLUE TIPS

In nature there always seems to be some time to waste.
I played with Ohio Blue-Tips waiting for the tea to boil.
Fire was a surprise. Fire is a surprise. Being so distinct, it can only be itself,
'not earth' 'not water' 'not air'. Being so itself it is quietly indestructible.

Like Bergman's *Virgin Spring*, with a blue film cast over it, the pines,
the grass, the picnic table black and white and blue. Oh the indestructible Max von Sydow
after the dull-witted thugs unable to comprehend his daughter's beauty
after the slaying builds a church to the God beyond suffering.

Max von Sydow continually building and rebuilding.
There is a blue fire in a man who must remake his ability to live,
cursed by both the action beyond his control and his own action. Silence,
that absence, is an action, a space qualified with implosion, fire.

Where does the heart go when it caves in, where does the mind go?
Raw material for the woodland cathedral that's superior to the city,
made with the exact earth where loss ruled and bit down the innocent wildly.
I'd be surprised now to sense it where we walk though the forest is capacious.

We miss renewal below the needle blanket and fern floor.
Quickly, quickly, we need the consolation in fire-treated stone.
Urgency is flattened as time goes rolling on, the weight of it.
But time too goes up in blue flame by the hour.

LAST POEM

His disciples said to him, "When will the new world come?" He said to them, "What you are looking forward to has come, but you don't know it."

(The Gospel of Thomas, verse 51)

Every fat green leaf on C Street lit with the end of the world.
Each leaf in the mind said that the apocalypse
already happened or was happening each moment
but went unnoticed. To be young astounds me now.
I'd forgotten the same fine cord was drawn
through then and now and later, the realization never ended.
The poem, the pen, the lamp, the cup
all slightly more than their forms, already out of their forms,
exposed to sight. The shoddy heft of supposed age
withers away, its withering space provides
ample room. And the joy of mind flows
through the joy of form
and gladness takes the cool, pure air
into its great lungs.
Such great and easy destruction.
I am rolled up within it.

ABOUT THE AUTHOR

Sean Norton received his MFA in Poetry from the University of Michigan and his BA from the University of Oregon after a couple of false starts at other schools. In the past he has taught poetry, fiction, and essay writing at the University of Michigan. Currently he works as an events planner.